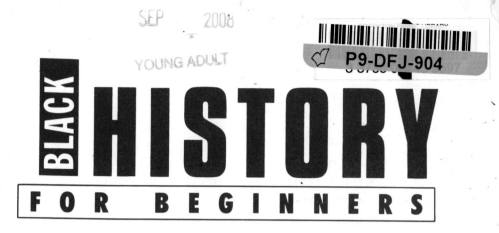

BLACK HISTORY
FOR BEGINNERS

DENISE DENNIS

ILLUSTRATED BY SUSAN WILLMARTH

For Beginners LLC
62 East Starrs Plain Road
Danbury, CT 06810 USA
www.forbeginnersbooks.com

Text: © 1984, 1995 Denise Dennis
Illustrations: © 1984, 1994 Susan Willmarth
Art Direction: Janet Siefert
Cover Design: Terrie Dunkelberger

A For Beginners® Documentary Comic Book
Originally published by Writers and Readers, Inc.
Copyright © 1984, 1995

Cataloging-in-publication information is available from the Library of Congress.

ISBN-10 # 1-934389-19-6 Trade
ISBN-13 # 978-1-934389-19-5 Trade

Manufactured in the United States of America

For Beginners® and Beginners Documentary Comic Books® are published by For Beginners LLC.

Reprint Edition

BLACK History
FOR BEGINNERS

"This is no time to engage in the luxury of cooling off or to take the tranquilizing drug of gradualism. Now is the time to make real the promises of democracy. Now is the time to make justice a reality for all of God's children."

Martin Luther King
August 28, 1963

When Washington crossed the Delaware, two blacks were with him.

5

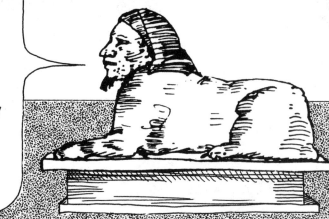

No. African history and black history aren't necessarily the same.

Black history is a separate branch of African history that extends beyond its borders.

7

Black history is the American history that was omitted from your textbooks.

Aesop, St. Augustine and Pushkin were of African heritage.

There are people of African descent throughout the world, from Indonesia to the Soviet Union.

9

But those who have waged the most enduring struggle for their rights are blacks in the nation that was founded on civil liberties, freedom and equality-- the United States of America.

The black quest in the United States has been the litmus paper on which the proclaimed ideals of the Declaration of Independence and the Constitution have been tested.

The results indicate that "LIBERTY AND JUSTICE FOR ALL" has been more fancy than fact.

Blacks were in the New World before Columbus arrived. They participated in the first explorations.

Blacks were in Cortéz's crew in Mexico, with Pizarro in Peru and Alvarado in Quito.

When Balboa discovered the Pacific Ocean, 30 blacks were with him, including Nufo de Olano.

When Alarcon and Coronado conquered New Mexico, blacks were with them, too.

The best-known of the black conquistadors was ESTIVANICO — he initiated the opening of New Mexico and Arizona for Spain.

el dorado

If there are misunderstandings between black and white people today, it's because misconceptions about blacks have been allowed to thrive.

The only way to help abolish stereotypes is to present a more complete picture of black people in history.

Native Americans in the Chicago area claimed that "The first white man to settle at Chickagoa was a negro."

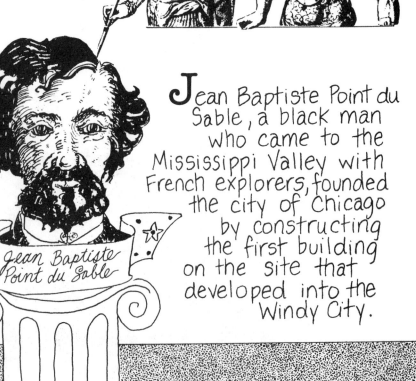

Jean Baptiste
Point du Sable

Jean Baptiste Point du Sable, a black man who came to the Mississippi Valley with French explorers, founded the city of Chicago by constructing the first building on the site that developed into the Windy City.

It's inspiring to know that blacks made a triumphant entrance into the Western World, but considering the circumstances of millions of blacks today, something went wrong...

Something called SLAVERY...

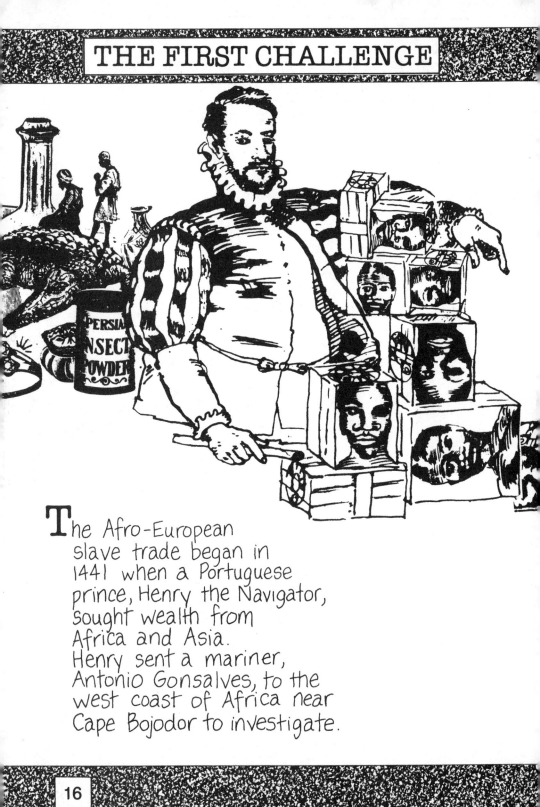

The Afro-European slave trade began in 1441 when a Portuguese prince, Henry the Navigator, sought wealth from Africa and Asia. Henry sent a mariner, Antonio Gonsalves, to the west coast of Africa near Cape Bojodor to investigate.

Gonsalves brought
gold dust and ten Africans
back to Lisbon for
the Prince, as a display of
Africa's wealth.

The Prince gave the
Africans to the Pope.

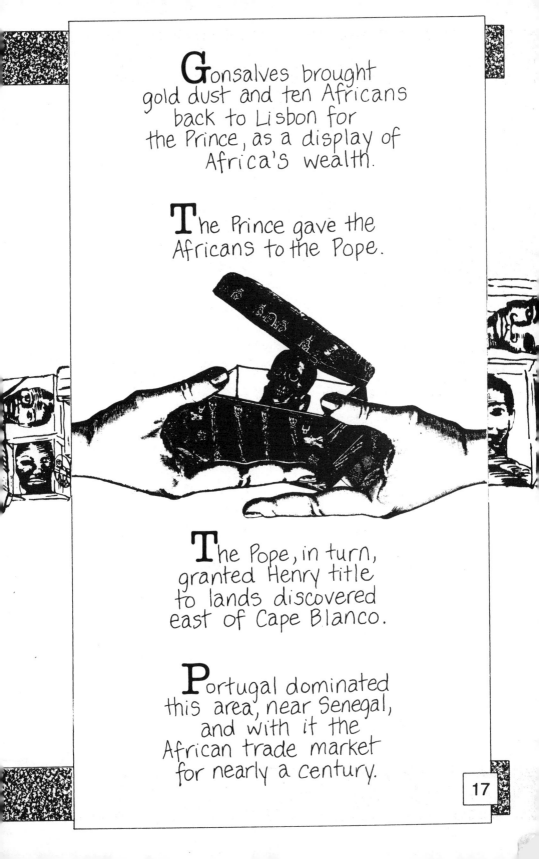

The Pope, in turn,
granted Henry title
to lands discovered
east of Cape Blanco.

Portugal dominated
this area, near Senegal,
and with it the
African trade market
for nearly a century.

A Papal Bull prevented Spain from going into Africa, but did give her the bulk of the New World. Spain contracted other nations to procure slaves for her. The contract was called an asiento and was a symbol of power.

By 1460, approximately 600 slaves were entering Portugal annually. In Lisbon, blacks outnumbered whites.

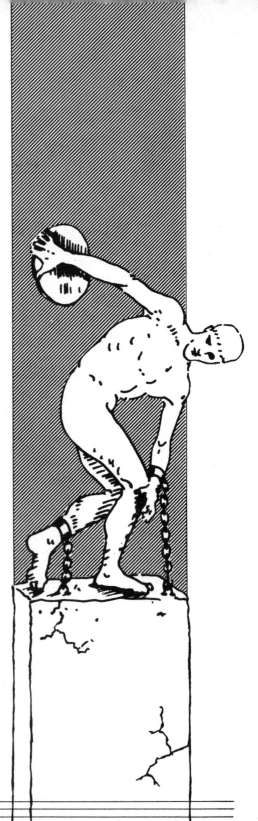

The Portuguese didn't invent slavery. For example, the ancient Greeks kept slaves and Moses led the Israelites out of bondage in Egypt.

On the west coast of the dark continent, a slave system was initiated and perpetuated for economic purposes. The Commercial Revolution offered Carte Blanche to those who sought to exploit in order to rise on the social and economic ladder.

There were three distinct stages on the journey from Africa to the New World:

1. Capture and conditioning in Africa.

2. The sea voyage, or "Middle Passage."

3. Seasoning in the West Indies.

European traders rationalized that slavery was a "holy cause" because it introduced heathens to Christianity.

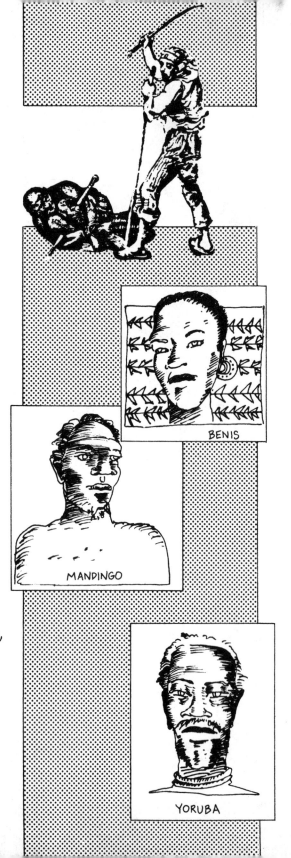

The roots of the slave trade:
The captured were members of various tribes. They were kidnapped or captured in tribal wars and sold. European traders established posts along the west African coastline where beads, guns, whiskey and ivory were bartered for bodies.

BENIS

MANDINGO

YORUBA

Men and women could be purchased from independent African *slatees*, too. Chiefs often appointed a *Caboceer*, an African who gathered those who were to be sold.

The *slatees* and the *Caboceer* led the capture in the long march to the coast-line. Those who were best fit physically were sought—the strong, brave and healthy.

After the long march the captured, chained two by two, were taken to negro "houses," or prison. The strongest were branded with the stamp of the trading company.

Incarceration in the "Negroe House" was followed by the chained march to the ship for the transatlantic voyage.

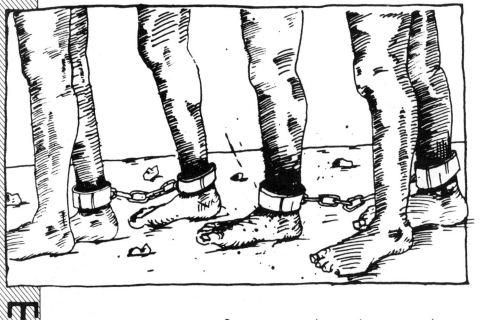

The journey lasted from eight to ten weeks. Many of the captured attempted to escape by jumping overboard. Others refused to eat. A slaveship's crew member often broke the teeth of the hunger strikers and force fed them. Loss of a black life meant loss of revenue.

The captured shared no common language. Some went mad in the claustrophobic quarters, others murdered those next to them in order to gain space.

Ship captains estimated that they would lose a percentage of African cargo in death via escape, suffocation, or illness. There was even insurrection insurance.

The "seasoning" period lasted from three to four years. Backs and spirits were broken in order to transform the Africans into American slaves.

They were trained by other slaves or by whites who had experience in "breaking in" even the most rebellious arrivals. Each slave was given a work assignment, repeating a task for twelve hours each day.

Any inclination toward suicide was beaten out of them. The death rate was high during the seasoning period because of the inability of slaves to adjust to the food or climate.

Absentee landlordism was responsible for the excess of brutality towards the slaves. Plantation owners entrusted their lands to overseers who saw slaves as beasts of burden.

In the 16th century 887,500 slaves were imported; in the 17th, 2,750,000; in the 18th, 7,000,000, and in the 19th, 3,250,000.

Slaves worked the sugar crop, which was shipped to New England, processed into rum, and then used to purchase more slaves in Africa.

Europeans turned the Caribbean into a slave-making factory.

J A M A I C A

By 1724, there were 32,000 blacks to 14,000 whites in Jamaica.

The high percentage of blacks gave rise to the strict black codes. The white populace feared insurrection knowing that in numbers, they were at a disadvantage. The sooner a slave accepted his or her helplessness, the better for those who sought to exploit.

In 1667, British Parliament adopted an "Act to regulate the Negroes on the British Plantations."

The Black Codes:

HIGHLIGHTS OF THIS ACT:

1. If a slave owner beats his slaves to death (or kills one by mistake) there shall be <u>no</u> legal repercussions.

2. All slaves must carry a pass at all times.

3. Slaves shall be whipped or branded on the face if they strike a "Christian."

4. "Christians" are not held responsible for destroying personal property (slaves).

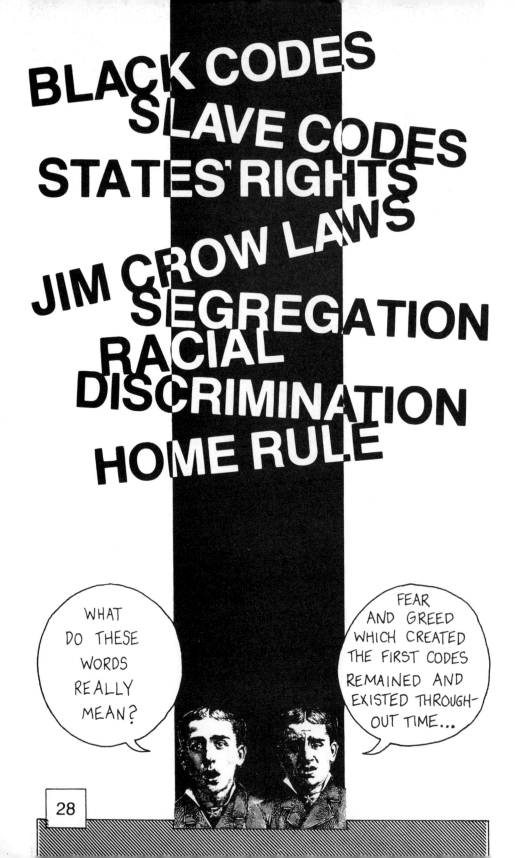

DATE	THE FEAR	THE SOLUTION
1667	High percentage of imported blacks & possible revolts.	BLACK CODES
1822 1831	Slaves like Vessey and Nat Turner rebel and kill whites.	SLAVE CODES
1865	·Post civil war slave holders in south want to remain "master."	HOME RULE
1886	Rutherford B. Hayes needs southern votes to win election.	STATES' RIGHTS
1896	Homer Plessey challenges legality of "separate but equal" railroad cars.	JIM CROW LAWS
1890's	Blacks try to better their lives using the ballot, education, organization and protest.	SEGREGATION AND DISCRIMINATION

The plantation owners and overseers had reason to fear the slaves rising against them, because slaves fought back whenever possible.

In 1522, there was a rebellion on the island of Santo Domingo and in 1526, the slaves in a settlement which was to become South Carolina revolted from the 500 Spaniards who held them.

Some of the blacks escaped to Haiti; others took refuge with Native Americans. Uprisings continued sporadically until the slaves were freed in the nineteenth century.

Two outstanding resisters of the black codes were Cudgo, a runaway slave in 18th-century Jamaica, and Macandal in Haiti. Both men led a group of runaways on their respective islands known as the Maroons. The Maroons lived in the island mountains and ignited revolts among the slaves. They gnawed at the planters' repressive system and intensified their fears.

Osecola, the Seminole chief.

Abraham, a black interpreter who lived with the Seminoles.

Caocoochee, a friend of fugitive slaves.

Now back to England in 1655...

Portugal was unable to maintain control of the slave trade. By 1655 England had won Jamaica from Spain and by the 18th century, held the *asiento*.

England dominated the industry. She supplied her colonies with slaves and indentured servants. The latter worked from four to seven years, at which time they were free to work for themselves.
Some were white ex-convicts from English prisons.

Slave trade centers shifted to places like Liverpool, England and Newport, Rhode Island.

The West Indies were depleted by constant sugar production. The soil was used up, and consequently the continents of North and South America became the primary production centers. In North America, tobacco was the attractive item, as it had been in the Caribbean.

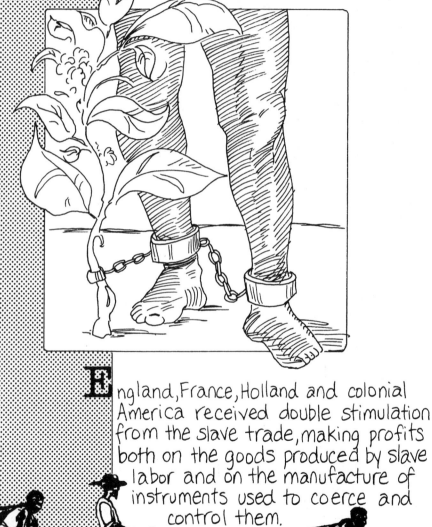

England, France, Holland and colonial America received double stimulation from the slave trade, making profits both on the goods produced by slave labor and on the manufacture of instruments used to coerce and control them.

By the late 1700's many slave ships were sailing directly to America from Africa ...

Major markets were set up in:

Newport, R.I.

Charleston, S.C.

Richmond, Va.

Philadelphia, Pa.

In the beginning, slavery wasn't confined to the Southern colonies. New Netherlands was founded by the Dutch West India Company, whose traffic was slaves. New York recognized slavery as legal in 1684. New Jersey, Delaware and Pennsylvania sanctioned the business, too. Massachusetts, Connecticut and Rhode Island condoned slavery.

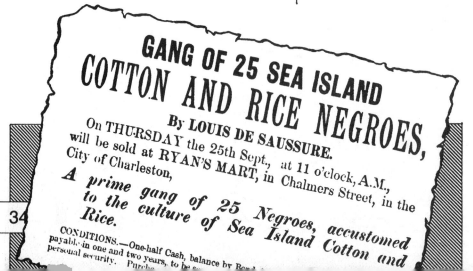

GANG OF 25 SEA ISLAND COTTON AND RICE NEGROES,

By LOUIS DE SAUSSURE.

On THURSDAY the 25th Sept., at 11 o'clock, A.M., will be sold at RYAN'S MART, in Chalmers Street, in the City of Charleston,

A prime gang of 25 Negroes, accustomed to the culture of Sea Island Cotton and Rice.

CONDITIONS.—One-half Cash, balance by Bo... payable in one and two years, to be s... personal security. Purcha...

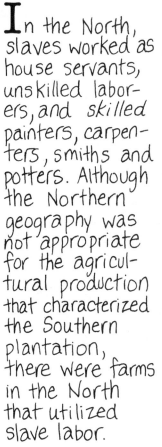

In the North, slaves worked as house servants, unskilled laborers, and *skilled* painters, carpenters, smiths and potters. Although the Northern geography was not appropriate for the agricultural production that characterized the Southern plantation, there were farms in the North that utilized slave labor.

In the New England Colonies, blacks were not more than 3% of the population, with the exception of Rhode Island, where they accounted for 10%. The slave codes in each of the colonies north and south were either severe or "lenient" depending on the percentage of blacks in the colony.

New England was the best place to be if you were a black slave.

Unlike the Southern slave owners, New England colonists placed no legal restrictions on educating slaves.

Slaves were guaranteed a fair trial, were allowed to testify against whites, and could sue.

In 1619, two black men, Antony and Pedro, a black woman, Isabella, and 17 additional blacks arrived at Jamestown, Virginia. They'd been "stolen" twice. Once from Africa, then from a Spanish cargo vessel en route to the Caribbean. A Dutch man-of-war took them from the Spanish and delivered them to Jamestown.

Little William the 1st

In 1624, a couple from that group were married. Their son, William Tucker, was the 1st black child born in the British colonies.

37

Taking their cue from the West Indies, Virginia planters began to appreciate the advantages in holding blacks to a lifetime of slavery. Black babies, unlike William Tucker, would be born with no opportunity for freedom.

Hmmm.....
let me figure this:

1 SLAVE LIFETIME
(minus minimum care costs)

+ 1 TOBACCO FIELD
(minus seed and crop transport)

= $ UNLIMITED PROFIT !!

In 1662, a Virginia law stated that a newborn was or was not free depending on the status of his mother.

Virginia subtly established statutes undermining the Negro population. For example, black servants were required to remain in service after their "indentured" time was over.

Baptism failed to alter or alleviate the slaves' condition.

According to the Virginia legislature, "conferring of baptisms doth not alter the condition of the person as to his bondage or freedome." New York, New Jersey, Maryland and the Carolinas adopted a similar policy by the early 1700's.

Spiritually, however, Christianity did offer them hope if not consolation. Black slaves absorbed the positive essence of Christianity. Faith and belief in an eventual promised land _on earth_ fed their imaginations and enabled them to persevere.

The mournfully deep spirituals express both personal emotions and understanding of the scriptures. Biblical allusions are consistent throughout the melodies. Spirituals like "Swing Low, Sweet Chariot" and "Deep River" betray overwhelming sorrow, such that death and the afterlife are perceived as joyous release.

The African musical heritage served more than a religious purpose.

African influences are united in the conga, rhumba and mambo. The tango is based on African rhythmic patterns, and its name is a derivate of an African word—"tangana." Brazil's samba is a descendant of the quizomba, the wedding dance of Angola.

Meanwhile, up North, Christian righteousness prevailed. Puritanism (which was originally synonymous with radicalism) and the Quaker Faith were the liberal left of the Colonies.

THE QUAKERS

George Keith of Philadelphia and his "friends" in the Society published the first antislavery document in the British colonies (1693). Even before this, in 1688, the Germantown protest took place, during which Quakers formally spoke against slavery.

Among the Quakers who were decidedly against slavery were the Society's founder, George Fox, Pennsylvania's founder, William Penn and John Woolman and Anthony Benezet, who wrote, printed and distributed anti-slavery literature.

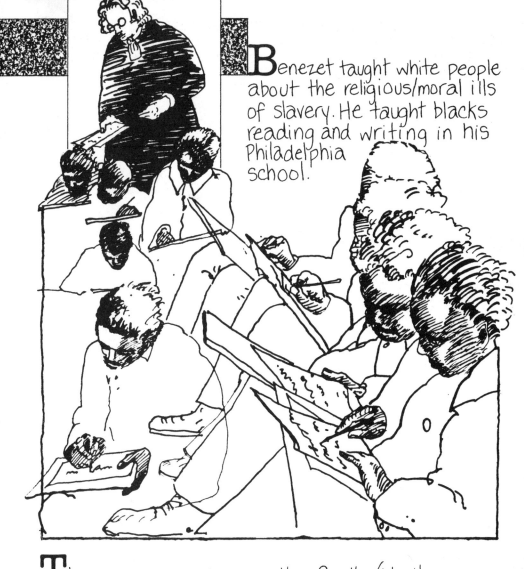

Benezet taught white people about the religious/moral ills of slavery. He taught blacks reading and writing in his Philadelphia school.

There were Quakers in the South (North Carolina) as well. By 1770, they were urging slaveholders to put an end to the "iniquitous practice."

QUAKERS WERE THE ORIGINAL FREEDOM RIDERS

NORTH CAROLINA OR BUST

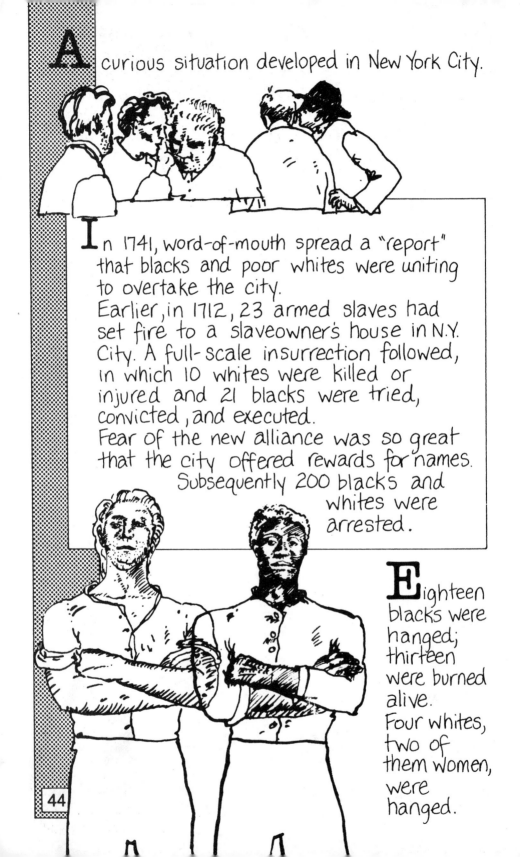

Acurious situation developed in New York City.

In 1741, word-of-mouth spread a "report" that blacks and poor whites were uniting to overtake the city.
Earlier, in 1712, 23 armed slaves had set fire to a slaveowner's house in N.Y. City. A full-scale insurrection followed, in which 10 whites were killed or injured and 21 blacks were tried, convicted, and executed.
Fear of the new alliance was so great that the city offered rewards for names. Subsequently 200 blacks and whites were arrested.

Eighteen blacks were hanged; thirteen were burned alive.
Four whites, two of them women, were hanged.

Efforts to divide these two groups and set them in competition for jobs, training and educational opportunities have persisted throughout American history.

On the eve of the American Revolution, there were slaves in all 13 colonies. Pennsylvania, with its strong Quaker influence, was regarded as the most humane and decent colony in respect to blacks. In 1780, it became the first state to abolish slavery.

CRISPUS ATTUCKS

Crispus Attucks of Massachusetts was one of the first to fall, and much has been made of that fact, but "blacks-and-the-American-Revolution" was more complex than a matter of one black man being shot at the beginning.

From New England, Abigail Adams pointed out to her Revolutionary husband:

"It has always appeared a most iniquitous scheme to me to fight ourselves for what we are daily robbing from those who have as good a right to freedom as we have."

Some blacks, like Gershom Prince of Pennsylvania, had already fought for the Colonies in the French and Indian War of 1763.

Blacks were for America; they sided with the Patriots against the Loyalists.

They were involved in the Stamp Act riots; when British troops were sent to Boston to intimidate the citizenry, blacks were among those who drove them out.

Black Revolutionaries

Many blacks fought at Bunker Hill, among them Prince Hall, P. Salem and Salem Poor.

Of Poor, the following commendation was made by his officers: "an experienced officer, as well as an excellent soldier... in the person of this said Negro centres a brave and gallant soldier."

A number of colonial legislatures passed their own anti-slave trade measures: Rhode Island and Connecticut in 1774. (Any slave entering Rhode Island was *automatically free.*) In 1773 Pennsylvania chose to put a £20 duty on each imported slave, which strongly discouraged trade. In the South, where fears were greatest, Virginia, North Carolina and Georgia passed laws which restricted the trade. These measures were a reaction to the vast number of physically fit blacks whose power could be overwhelming.

In his original draft of the Declaration of Independence Thomas Jefferson spoke against slavery in his indictment of George III:

"He has waged cruel war against human nature itself, violating its most sacred rights of life and liberty in the persons of a distant people who never offended him..."

If there was any doubt about the route slavery would take if the Revolution succeeded, that doubt was erased by the Continental Congress's reaction to the antislavery clause.

49

The Southern delegates, whose livelihood depended on slaves as both investments and laborers, perked up their ears when the clause was read. They refused to sign a declaration that made black slaves free and equal. The Continental Congress needed to present a united front. Without the Southern delegates it would have been weakened. The anti-slavery clause was not sufficient reason to lose them—in order to pacify the Southern delegates and sustain the union, the clause was excised.

The fear of possible uprisings proved to be an obstacle when it came to enlisting blacks for the American struggle.

In spite of the role of blacks in the French and Indian war and early battles with British troops, General George Washington issued an order that:

"... any stroller, negro or vagabond WILL NOT be recruited for service..."
~July 6, 1775

The British were more shrewd: In November 1775 Lord Dunmore, the governor of Virginia, issued another order freeing "all indentured servants...who would join his Majesty's service."

By January 1776, Washington issued another statement:

ALL BLACKS WHO HAVE ALREADY SERVED MAY RE-ENLIST

In Virginia alone, 31,000 or more slaves ran away. "Masters" did all they could to block them. After the war, the British evacuated more than 10,000 Negroes who set sail for England—despite Washington's objections.

By the end of the war 5000 blacks had served on the American side. Because free blacks were preferable to armed slaves, the majority of those who served were from the North.

Founding fathers like Benjamin Franklin and Benjamin Rush spoke against slavery after the war, as did many others.

Some progress was made:
- 1780-1786: Pennsylvania, Massachusetts, Connecticut, Rhode Island, New York and New Jersey passed manumission (freedom from slavery) acts.
- 1787: Congress added a provision to the Northwest Ordinance that slavery could not exist in territories under the ordinance.

The Constitutional Convention, however, dealt antislavery hopes a painful blow:
Slavery was recognized by the convention.

The pro-slavery sentiments were so strong that Ben Franklin did not even attempt to read the Pennsylvania Abolition Society's statement.

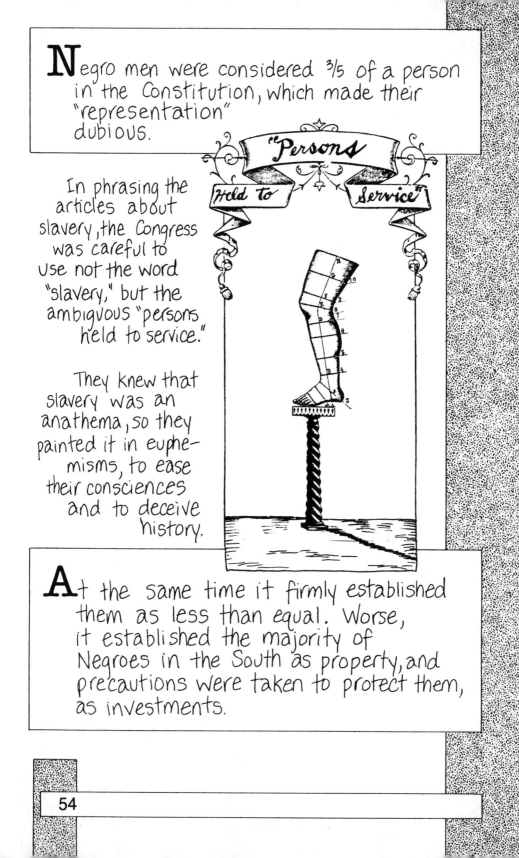

Negro men were considered ⅗ of a person in the Constitution, which made their "representation" dubious.

In phrasing the articles about slavery, the Congress was careful to use not the word "slavery," but the ambiguous "persons held to service."

They knew that slavery was an anathema, so they painted it in euphemisms, to ease their consciences and to deceive history.

"Persons Held to Service"

At the same time it firmly established them as less than equal. Worse, it established the majority of Negroes in the South as property, and precautions were taken to protect them, as investments.

The Constitutional Congress extended slavery twenty years as stipulated in Article II, Section 9: "... [slavery] shall not be prohibited by the Congress prior to the year [1808]..." Finally--one more blow-- Article IV: Congress passed a law which required states to return fugitive slaves to their owners.

The war rhetoric and the Quaker regard for human rights had little influence on the designers of the United States. By 1790, the total investment in slaves was $ 104,639,000.

"GOVERNMENT SHOULD REST ON THE DOMINION OF PROPERTY."
-U.S. CONGRESS, 1790

Or, as Calvin Coolidge said about 150 years later, "the business of America is business.

In the aftermath of the War for Independence, the plight of blacks had not changed.

FOR A WHILE IT SEEMED THAT SLAVERY MIGHT DIE BECAUSE TOBACCO WAS NO LONGER IN DEMAND...

Industrially advanced England was opening doors for a new product--cotton.

Cotton

Machines to spin and weave raw cotton fiber revolutionized manufacturing. Cotton seed had to be separated from the fiber before it could be used.

The Southern soil was a "natural" for growing cotton. Cultivating it required the kind of monotonous labor "masters" thought ideal for slaves. Busy slaves meant that their "investments" in human lives would be saved--property protected. Southern planters needed to find a way to separate those cotton seeds.

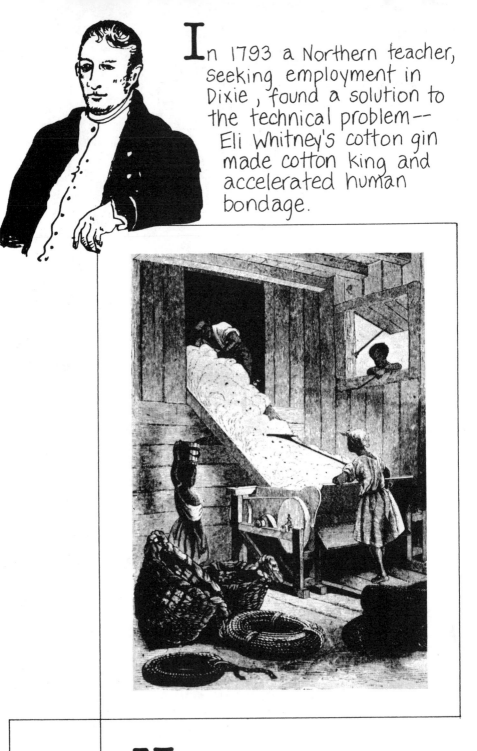

In 1793 a Northern teacher, seeking employment in Dixie, found a solution to the technical problem-- Eli Whitney's cotton gin made cotton king and accelerated human bondage.

New England merchants provided slaves for Southern plantations.

The violation of black woman slaves was not illegal. If a man molested a slave belonging to another, then the crime was in "damaging the property."

The children of mixed unions kept the status of their mothers —slaves. Some slaveholders kept their own off-spring in perpetual servitude while others freed them.

Archibald McMillan freed a woman and her five children.

"FOR THE FAITHFUL SERVICE SHE HAS RENDERED ME — THE OTHERS I FREE ON ACCOUNT OF BELIEVING THEM TO BE MY OWN CHILDREN."

59

By the 1870's many newly freed slaves had more white than Negro blood--

SLAVE GROUP FROM LOUISIANA

Thomas Jefferson devised a mathematical formula to determine what percentage of Negro blood made a child of mixed parentage a Negro.

The categories divided into:

— MULATTO (½)

— QUADROON (¼)

— OCTOROON (⅛)

There were two groups of slaves--those in the field and those in the main house. This created a hierarchy.

The slave who held most authority was the "driver," who worked for the overseer. His job was to supervise the field hands-- making sure they worked incessantly, punishing idlers with a whip.

Field slaves worked long hours under the sun. They lived in huts and slept on mats on the floor, and had two sets of clothing: fall and spring, and a heavy blanket every third year.

House slaves ran the master's house-- cleaned, cooked, brought children into the world and nursed them. They lived more comfortably than their fieldhand brethren.

Because they were closer to the "massa," house slaves weren't trusted by those in the field.

Dividing blacks and making them distrustful of one another was one way to maintain control.

More divisive was the attempt to weaken the slaves' unity by breaking up families. Slave marriages were not recognized as legal.

Slaves created their own ceremonies: jumping over the broomstick was a ritual symbolizing the couple's jump into matrimony.

Children were sold and separated from their parents. The family, a nucleus of strength, was subject to the market place and the whims of the master.

If a slave mother delivered a child at the same time as the mistress of the plantation, she had to nurse the white child rather than her own.

Since slaves were a commodity on the market, like cattle, breeding slaves was a lucrative practice. Plantation records list the births of slaves under "stock."

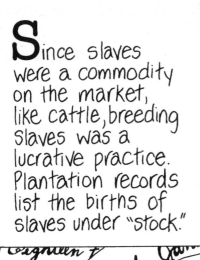

Myths about the "ole South" picture all plantations as large with hundreds of slaves.

There were about 20 slaves on the average plantation. Most employed about 5 slaves. About 10,000 plantations had 50 or more slaves, and only a quarter of all Southern slaves worked on the large estates.

REVOLTS FOR FREEDOM

There are more than 250 slave revolts on record. Rebellion went hand in hand with slavery. Some slaves fought back, ran away, poisoned the owner, even burned buildings. Others worked very, very slowly at a task. The most dreaded act of dissension was that of open revolt.

Gabriel Prosser was a slave from Henrico County, Virginia. He and his co-conspirators collected guns and swords in a plan to take over the Richmond arsenal. Two slaves revealed the details to their masters. The government was alerted and the state militia was prepared. Prosser and thirty-four others were convicted and hanged.

Twenty-two years later—1822, Denmark Vesey prepared his revolt. In 1800, Vesey purchased his freedom and worked as a carpenter in Charleston, South Carolina. He managed money well, bought property, and was well-respected.

Vesey weaved his scheme over a period of years, talking to slaves about human rights and the need to fight for freedom at all costs. He was persuasive and brought an estimated 9,000 blacks into his plan. He selected his assistants cautiously, and set the date for July 1822.

Aware that house servants were not to be trusted, they took precautions so that none would be informed. One conspirator, however, tried to convince a house slave to join the revolt, and that slave informed. The leaders were executed and four white men were imprisoned for assisting the blacks involved in Vesey's plot.

Nat Turner believed he was chosen by God to lead his people from bondage.

The solar eclipse in February 1831 was signifi-cant enough to tell him that the time for action had arrived. The county seat was in Jerusalem--and Nat read that as a direct command from the scriptures. He planned the revolt for July 4th, but when he became ill, he waited for another divine signal.

His sign came on August 13, when the sun turned. Nat rescheduled the revolt for the 21st. The reign of terror was swift. Beginning with Nat's master and his family, sixty whites were killed within twenty-four hours. The next day, state and federal troops arrived to stop the bloody revolt.

Turner was executed on November 11. His uprising was a "signal" that things had reached a peak. Abolitionists had evidence that theirs was a cause that must be won. It was to be a fight to the finish.

67

Southerners responded by intensifying the Slave Codes.

Slaves CAN NOT:

- Assemble in groups of more than 5.
- Own property or testify in court.
- Strike a white.
- Learn to read & write or to buy & sell goods.
- Conduct religious service without a white present.
- Possess firearms.
- Beat drums.
- Etc., etc., etc.!!!

WHAT, MORE CODES?!

In 1831, the year of Nat Turner's revolt, the New England Anti-slavery society was formed by William Lloyd Garrison. In 1833, the American Anti-slavery Society was organized in Philadelphia, with Arthur Tappan of New York as its first president. State and local organizations spoke and published literature against slavery.

David Walker, a free Boston black, published his "Appeal."

The Underground Railroad was an organized escape system for runaway slaves.

It operated at night, following the Northern Star, and was run by *conductors* who met and accompanied the runaways. The main states involved were Ohio, Indiana, Pennsylvania, Delaware, and Maryland. *Stations* were 10–20 miles apart, and covered wagons, wagons with false bottoms, and closed carriages were used. During the day, fugitives were hidden in barns, attics and haylofts. Men, women and children escaped via the railroad without rails.

It was a daring enterprise, with more than 3,200 people involved in its operation. **Between 1830 and 1860 approximately 2,500 slaves per year "rode" to freedom.**

Harriet Tubman was the Railroad's "Scarlet Pimpernel."

She freed herself, returned to free her family, then made 19 additional trips south. Via "General Moses" strategy, more than 300 slaves were conducted to freedom in Canada.

Quakers and philanthropic organizations in Philadelphia and New York raised money for the railroad. Harriet Tubman did domestic work to earn money when necessary. More than 3,000 slaves escaped on the Underground Railroad, defying fugitive slave laws.

This tiny, brave woman later became a nurse, spy and scout during the Civil War.

Women were active in the anti-slavery movement.

Several women who became leaders of the suffrage movement were abolition activists: Lucretia Mott, Susan B. Anthony, Elizabeth Cady Stanton.

Harriet Beecher Stowe wrote <u>Uncle Tom's Cabin</u> in reaction to the outrageous Fugitive Slave Act.

Prudence Crandall opened a school for Negro girls in her Canterbury, Connecticut home.

The townspeople had her arrested.

Frederick Augustus Washington Bailey was a slave who escaped, changed his name and went on to be the most articulate spokesman of the anti-slavery cause-- Frederick Douglass.

In 1847, Frederick Douglass published his weekly paper, "The North Star."

STATES, SLAVES, THE STAKES

The period from 1800 until the onset of the Civil War in 1860 was marked by legislation concerning slavery:

1820 MISSOURI COMPROMISE

Prohibited slavery in the Kansas-Nebraska Territory.

1842 PRIG VS. PENNSYLVANIA

A blow for slaveholders –the Supreme Court ruled that state officials were not authorized to return fugitive slaves to their owners.

1850 COMPROMISE OF 1850

California entered the Union as a free state; other territories entered with no decision on slavery; Texas ceded lands to Mexico with compensation; a stricter fugitive slave law to protect slaveholders; slave trade prohibited in Washington, D.C.

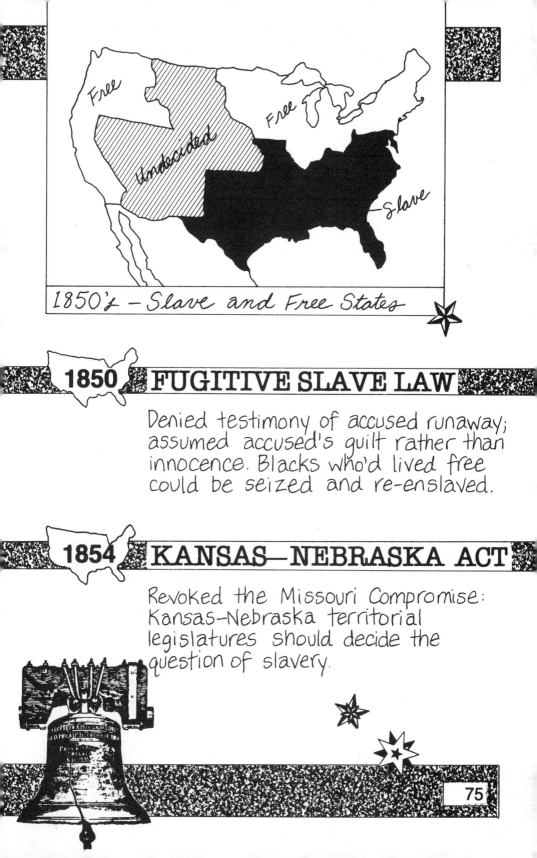

1850's – Slave and Free States

1850 FUGITIVE SLAVE LAW

Denied testimony of accused runaway; assumed accused's guilt rather than innocence. Blacks who'd lived free could be seized and re-enslaved.

1854 KANSAS—NEBRASKA ACT

Revoked the Missouri Compromise: Kansas-Nebraska territorial legislatures should decide the question of slavery.

Scott, a former slave who had lived in free states for a number of years, sued his former "master" for his freedom. The Supreme Court ruled that Negroes were <u>not</u> U.S. Citizens and therefore could not take a case to court.

"THE SUPREME COURT IS NOT THE ONLY POWER IN THE WORLD... TANEY CANNOT BAIL OUT THE OCEAN ... OR PLUCK THE STAR OF LIBERTY FROM THE NORTHERN SKY"
—FREDERICK DOUGLASS

"NEGROES HAVE NO RIGHTS WHICH THE WHITE MAN IS BOUND TO RESPECT"
—JUSTICE TANEY

The following excerpt is from a letter written by the French author Alexandre Dumas (The Count of Monte Cristo, The Three Musketeers) to a Southern Democrat:

> Paris 1847
>
> Sir,
>
> My mother was a negro and I am not ashamed to confess that my person makes open declaration of my lineage... I am anxious to visit your country... One thing deters me... I am told that my African blood will subject me to inconvenience in your country, and that I may even be taken and sold as a slave, according to existing laws.

On October 16th, 1859 John Brown raided the arsenal at Harper's Ferry, Virginia in hope of leading a slave insurrection. Fifty men were in his group. Of the five black men involved, one survived.

The South tried to portray Brown as a maniac. He was hanged on December 2, 1859.

At a meeting commemorating John Brown's death a riot broke out and Frederick Douglass was flung down the steps of Fremont Temple in Boston.

The events of 1800–1859 culminated in the following events:

1. The birth of the Republican Party (anti-slavery platform)

2. The election of President Abraham Lincoln

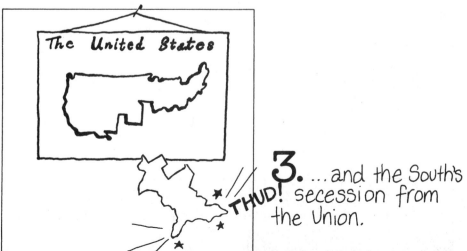

THUD!

3. ...and the South's secession from the Union.

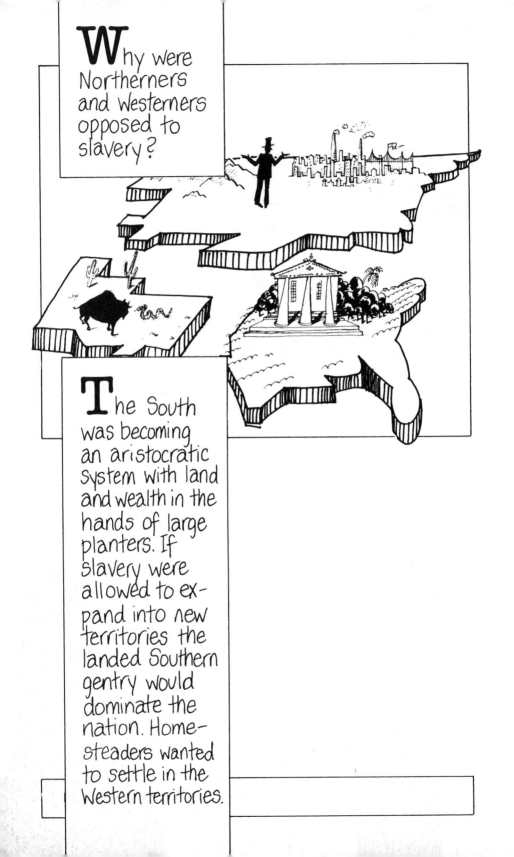

Why were Northerners and Westerners opposed to slavery?

The South was becoming an aristocratic system with land and wealth in the hands of large planters. If slavery were allowed to expand into new territories the landed Southern gentry would dominate the nation. Home-steaders wanted to settle in the Western territories.

Compromises with the South were an attempt to appease and keep the Union together.

Northern manufacturers and New York businessmen depended on Southern trade.

New York City was decidedly anti-Lincoln in 1860. Rumors abounded that New York City would secede with the South and set itself up as a port to carry on trade between Great Britain and the Confederates.

This never came about. Although England sympathized with the South, there were anti-slavery sentiments in Britain. New York fought for the Union; however, there were many Copperheads (Northerners who sympathized with the South) active in New York City.

Initially, Lincoln wanted to abolish slavery by establishing a colony for former slaves in Liberia or the West Indies. The scheme was unsuccessful.

When the South seceded from the Union it was rebellion against the United States.

Lincoln went to war to preserve the Union and he used the _opportunity_ of war to free the slaves.

By the time he signed the Emancipation Proclamation on January 1, 1863, the nation was two years into the war.

He freed slaves in the states that seceded (destroying their supply of free labor) but not those in the border states (slave states that did not secede).

800,000 slaves remained unfree!

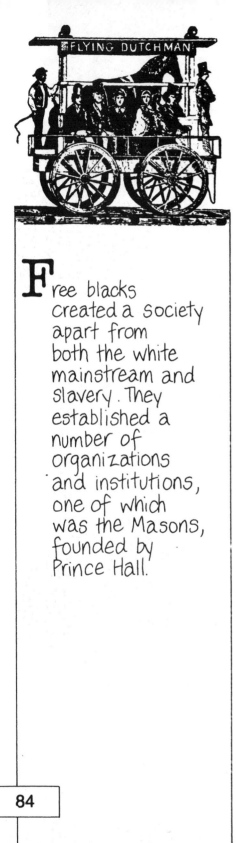

Free blacks created a society apart from both the white mainstream and slavery. They established a number of organizations and institutions, one of which was the Masons, founded by Prince Hall.

Two devout Christians in Philadelphia, Absolom Jones and Richard Allen, founded black churches after they were instructed to move to the "colored section" of a Methodist church-- while their heads were bowed in prayer.

Richard Allen's Bethel African Methodist Church (1816) spread throughout Pennsylvania and eventually became one of the strongest black institutions in the country.

ABSOLOM JONES

RICHARD ALLEN

The first Negro Baptist Church, Savannah, Georgia.

The African Methodist Episcopal Zion Church was founded in New York City in 1821. The Baptist Church was another influential institution among blacks.

The churches were often the educational, social and civic nucleus of the free Negroes' life, a tradition that continued into the next century. Black churches have been the black national network.

In early 1861, Frederick Douglass was considering colonizing American Negroes in Haiti, fearing that Lincoln would not act to abolish slavery.

The Confederates, however, did him a favor: on April 12, 1861, they fired on Fort Sumter in South Carolina and seceded—the war was on!

Negroes immediately started flooding into the Union camps -- in the North they were ready to enlist; in the South, they fled to fight for freedom. Union officers in Dixie did not know what to do with the sea of dark faces. General Ben Butler declared them "contraband of war" (still property!) and put them in camps where they worked for the army.

"Slavery is a moral evil in any society ... more so to the white than to the black... I believe in the Union...

ROBERT E. LEE

One Union officer declared slaves of the Missouri Confederates free, but Lincoln declared it invalid.

He also declared that:

Negroes could not enlist or fight in the war -- despite the Negro military units, like the Hannibal Guards of Pennsylvania and the Crispus Attucks Guard of Ohio that organized when the war began. Blacks repeatedly offered their services to the War Department and were turned down.

Lincoln wanted to keep "the Negro question" out of the war and he didn't want to offend the border states.

No consistent policy was established, and many fugitive slaves were returned from the Union to their masters.

The rebels weren't worried about offending anyone—while Lincoln dilly-dallied about using Negroes, the Rebs used their slaves to work for *their* war effort.

Slaves kept the plantations running while "massa" went to fight to make sure they remained enslaved.

When Lincoln *finally* realized that slaves were being used against the Union, the Confiscation Act (Aug. 6, 1861) was passed. It stated that any property used in rebellion against the U.S. would lawfully belong to the country. If said property were slaves, they would be free. ("Persons of African descent" were made available to the President as needed.)

Following this, thousands of Negroes migrated to Union camps in the South, but the conditions in the camps were poor—many died from hunger. Free, yes—but with no land, money, or place in the scheme of things. This problem was magnified after the war.

By late 1862, Lincoln consented to enlist Negroes (The Militia Act).

Official recruitment began in 1863. On the heels of the Emancipation Proclamation, the War Department initiated the Bureau of Colored Troops.

Until 1864, black soldiers were paid $7 per month; whites, $13 per month. In Massachusetts the all-black 54th Regiment served a year without pay rather than accept the discriminating wage.

156,000

black troops fought for the Union Army in 449 operations and 39 major battles.

22 received
the congressional medal of honor.

39,000

blacks were in the Union Navy and approximately 200,000 volunteered in non-military capacities.

In December of 1863 Lincoln devised a plan to rebuild the economic and political South and to aid the 4 million former slaves in beginning their lives as free people.

The Freeman's Bureau (1865-72) was set up under General Howard to meet the needs of Negroes.

The first task was to secure economic freedom for blacks.

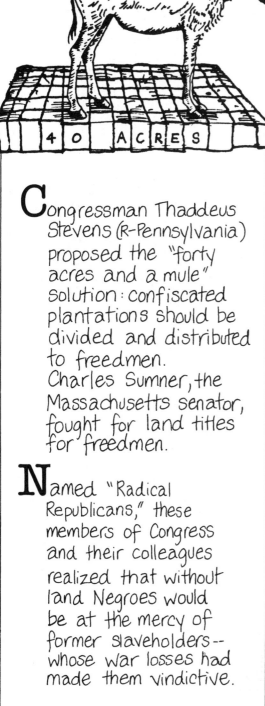

4 0 ACRES

Congressman Thaddeus Stevens (R-Pennsylvania) proposed the "forty acres and a mule" solution: confiscated plantations should be divided and distributed to freedmen. Charles Sumner, the Massachusetts senator, fought for land titles for freedmen.

Named "Radical Republicans," these members of Congress and their colleagues realized that without land Negroes would be at the mercy of former slaveholders -- whose war losses had made them vindictive.

President Andrew Johnson,
anxious to make amends with
former rebels, pardoned them,
returned their lands, and
granted home rule,
which meant
white home rule.

HOME RULE

Let's make a deal

Fearing economic and political
gains by blacks, a revised
edition of
Black Codes
was designed.

NOT AGAIN!

Βut an amazing thing happened next--
THE BLACK CODES BACKFIRED!!

The 39th Congress, controlled by Republicans, refused to recognize the Southern Delegates who intended to institutionalize a modified form of slavery. "The Joint Committee of Fifteen," led by Stevens and Sumner, was appointed to investigate the ex-Confederate states.

Their findings helped sway public opinion and Congress to pass a Civil Rights Act (April 1866) that gave slaves citizenship. In June 1866, Congress passed the Fourteenth Amendment, which gave blacks the ballot.

Civil Rights Act: PASSED April 1866

14th Amendment BLACKS GET VOTING RIGHTS: JUNE 1866

In the South, only Tennessee ratified the measure. The other states reacted with reprisals against blacks -- riots and the burning of black schools and churches.

Congress responded with the Reconstruction Act (March 2, 1867). The former Confederate States (except Tennessee) were divided into five districts and placed under martial law. The states were required to ratify the Fourteenth Amendment in order to be readmitted.

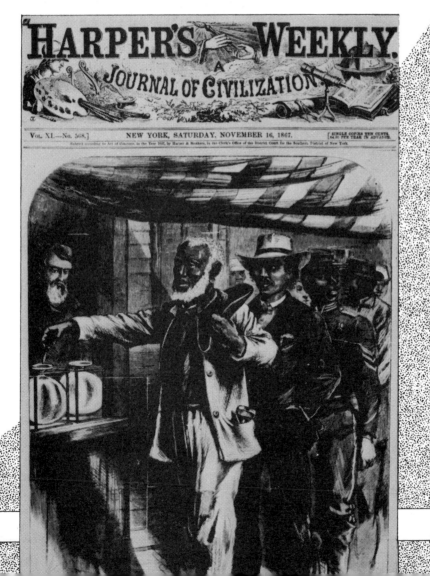

Black voters gave the Republicans a political advantage.

They organized the Loyal League, an outgrowth of the northern Union League--aimed at securing the black ballot. On March 5, 1870, the 15th Amendment was passed to protect black suffrage.

During this optimistic period, many blacks were elected or appointed to government: between 1868 and 1896, 113 black legislators served in Louisiana alone.

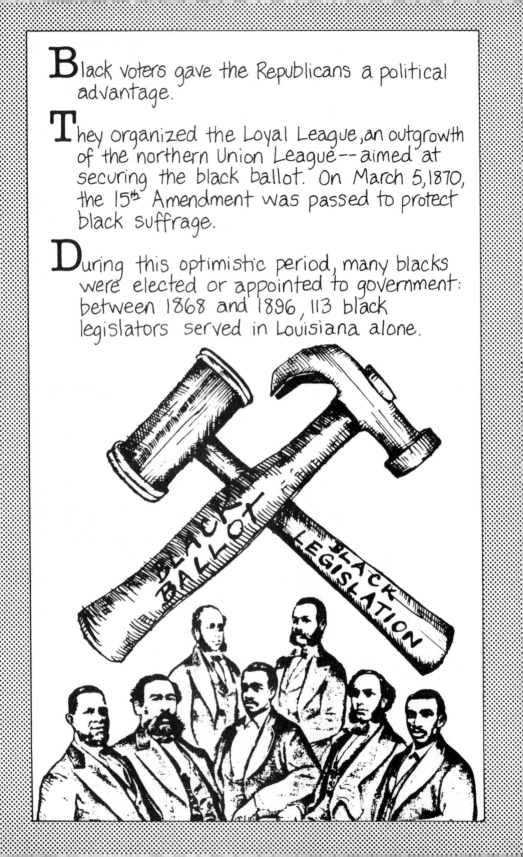

Freedmen as Legislators:

In the "reconstructed" South Carolina legislature, 50 members were black and 13 white. Most were former slaves who learned to read and write while in office.

The power of the black vote was evident in the 1868 Presidential election. 450,000 blacks voted for Grant: the Democratic candidate lost by 300,000. **Blacks gave Grant the decisive edge.**

Under President Ulysses S. Grant's administration Reconstruction flourished. New England school teachers moved south and opened schools for black children with government funding. Morehouse College, Fisk and Howard Universities were born. The Freedman's Bureau spent five million dollars on educating blacks.

Southern backlash unleashed its fangs with a vengeance.

Terrorist groups like the Ku Klux Klan resorted to lynching, tar-and feathering, whipping, threats, and burning homes.

Blacks were prevented from voting by stuffed ballot boxes, hidden sites, and by being arrested right before election day.

Disenfranchisement was ultimately accomplished in 1898 through the "grand-father clause" poll tax and by the administration of "literacy tests"—contrivances to get around the Fifteenth Amendment.

Southern Democrats were on a rampage to recapture their lost power.

Reconstruction ended in 1877.

Its demise was sealed by the election of Rutherford B. Hayes (1876) who cuddled up to the white South in order to "buy" the electoral votes he needed.

The bargain gave certain states "the right to control their own affairs in their own way," better known as states' rights.

Thaddeus Stevens died in 1868 and, at his request, was buried in a Negro cemetery, where "all God's children are equal."

Charles Sumner was working for a Civil Rights Bill to prohibit discrimination and segregation in schools and public places when he died in 1874.

With States' Rights came Jim Crow laws, or "radical discrimination."

In 1883, Sumner's Civil Rights Act of 1875 was declared unconstitutional by the Supreme Court.

The final downhill slide came in 1896 in the Plessy vs. Ferguson decision.

Homer Plessy challenged a Louisiana railroad's forcing him to sit in a "separate but equal" car, charging that it was a violation of his constitutional rights.

Justice John Marshall Harlan
spoke on Plessy's behalf:

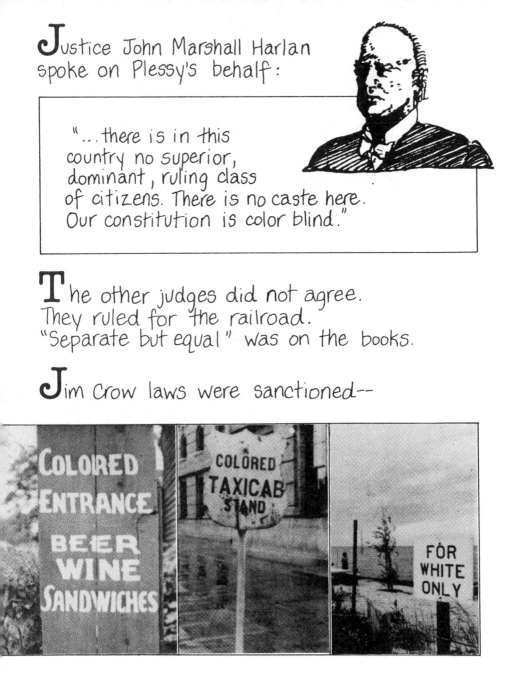

"... there is in this
country no superior,
dominant, ruling class
of citizens. There is no caste here.
Our constitution is color blind."

The other judges did not agree.
They ruled for the railroad.
"Separate but equal" was on the books.

Jim Crow laws were sanctioned--

COLORED
ENTRANCE
BEER
WINE
SANDWICHES

COLORED
TAXICAB
STAND

FOR
WHITE
ONLY

--in public transportation,
stores, post offices,
drinking fountains,
and libraries.

Until the 1940's the American Red Cross kept negro blood segregated in blood banks.

Undaunted blacks in the South developed another tool for rebuilding their lives: EDUCATION.

Black colleges founded during the second half of the nineteenth century continue to provide needed opportunities for young black people. Among them are Atlanta University, Virginia Union, Spelman, Hampton Institute and Clark.

In 1944, the United Negro College Fund was established to ensure the continued success of black colleges and universities.

Booker T. Washington founded Tuskegee Institute in Alabama in 1881. He believed that the most practical training for Negroes was vocational. This philosophy made him popular among philanthropists. At the 1895 Atlanta Expo, he compared black/white relations to fingers:

"WE CAN BE AS SEPARATE AS THE FINGERS, YET ONE AS THE HAND."

Was he endorsing Jim Crow? It seemed that way.
He urged blacks and whites to cast their buckets where they were. Blacks, he felt, were better off accepting existing conditions and gradually changing them by acquiring skills.

W.E.B. DuBois disagreed with Washington's approach to education. A Harvard graduate, DuBois believed that blacks should have access to higher education. His theory was that "the talented tenth," blacks who'd had educational advantages, should teach others.

He felt that Booker T. Washington was obliging white racists and, by restricting black occupations to trades, perpetuating the idea of "inferiority."
Where Washington accommodated, DuBois refused to accommodate.

There were no official Jim Crow laws in the North, but blacks were still the last hired and first fired. Both European immigrants and blacks were subject to an industrialized version of sharecropping.

In the South, sharecropping replaced slavery. Destitute blacks and whites sold their labor to planters for a "share" of the crop.

The planter sold cabins, work animals and tools, food, clothes and other supplies to them on credit. At season's end, the share-cropper would pay his debts with profits from the crop.

Sounds fair—but it wasn't. Planters charged whatever they liked and added interest.

Farmers were encouraged to overspend. The result was a quicksand of debt that became deeper each season.

Their wages kept them alive, but they could do nothing to better their impoverished conditions.

This brought about two phenomenon: Black Migration to the North and The Populist Movement.

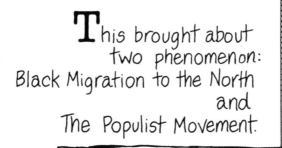

All Colored People

THAT WANT TO

GO TO KANSAS,

On September 5th, 1877,

Can do so for $5.00

In 1879, Benjamin Singleton, "Pap" to his friends, led more than 40,000 black sharecroppers to Kansas. Many made the journey on foot.

The South was no place for blacks, so many migrated north and west in hopes of finding a better way of life.

Planters and businessmen were upset by the loss of cheap labor, so Congress investigated to find out why blacks were leaving Dixie.

They decided the primary cause was working conditions.

Within ten years, 100,000 blacks migrated to Texas. Black cowboys were legendary. They drove cattle, scouted and mined for gold.

Negroes traveled as far west as Oregon and California. They founded Boley, Langston and Summit -- all black towns in Oklahoma.

The most famous black cowboys were Nat Love, nicknamed "Deadwood Dick" for the riding and marksmanship contest he won at Deadwood, Dakota in 1876, and Bill Pickett, the "Dusty Demon," who is in the Cowboy Hall of Fame.

Meanwhile, oppression continued South of the Mason-Dixon line:

The Populist Movement was an attempt to unite blacks and poor whites politically. They denounced lynchings and tried to help both races to recognize their common bond.

The Populists failed, in part, because poor whites nursed their racism: blacks (in their minds) kept them from being the lowest on the socioeconomic totem pole.

"Our progress has never depended on the President or Congress... it has always depended on the action of black people and the power of God."

Andrew Young
1982

Blacks entered into the 20th century armed with a new weapon:

ORGANIZATION.

In 1905, the Niagara Movement met at Niagara Falls, Canada, with W.E.B. DuBois as its leader. They were considered radical because they vehemently demanded action rather than empty promises.

Members of the Niagara Movement became part of a new organization.

In 1910, the

National

Association for the

Advancement of

Colored

People

was founded.

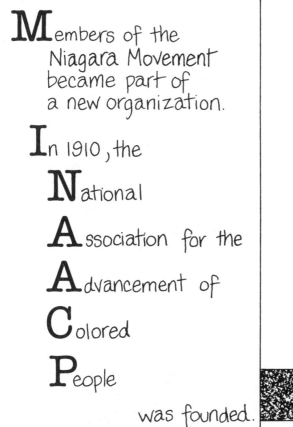

Inspired by Mary White Ovington, a group was organized by William English Walling, a white writer, and Oswald Garrison Villard, the abolitionist's grandson. The group (including Jane Addams, Ida B. Wells, William Dean Howells, and John Dewey) was committed to upholding Negro suffrage and ending discrimination.

DuBois was responsible for the NAACP's publication, **Crisis.** The NAACP worked through the legal system, taking cases to courts.

In 1911 the **National League** was organized to help Negroes who were entering urban centers. Housing, jobs, practical information about city life, and social work training were made available.

As we have seen, blacks have a history of military participation.

In 1898, when the *Maine* blew up at the beginning of the Spanish-American War, 30 blacks were on board. That same year, Teddy Roosevelt's Rough Riders charged up San Juan Hill, after the all-black 9th and 10th Cavalries opened the way for them.

Roosevelt was impressed enough to say:

WELL, THE 9TH AND 10TH MEN ARE ALL RIGHT! THEY CAN DRINK OUT OF OUR CANTEENS...

The first person to be drafted under the new selective service was a black man: Leo A. Pinckney.

Washington officials promised the NAACP an officers training camp if 200 black college men could be recruited--15,000 volunteered. Des Moines, Iowa, became the camp site and in October 1917, 639 blacks became commissioned officers in the United States Army.

Negroes, however, were barred from the Marines and could not become officers in the Navy.

SEARGEANT HENRY JOHNSON

NEEDHAM ROBERTS

Two members of the all-black 369ᵗʰ infantry, Henry Johnson and Needham Roberts, were awarded the French Croix de guerre for aborting a surprise German attack. The two men killed or wounded more than 20 enemy soldiers... the incident was named "Henry Johnson's War."

Lieutenant J.R. Europe and his 39ᵗʰ Regimental Band were credited for introducing jazz to the French.

The Germans took advantage of U.S. racial tensions and distributed flyers among Negro troops overseas: "Do you enjoy the same rights as the white people do in America?"

CENTENAIRE DE 1789

REPUBLIQUE FRANÇAISE

The American government distributed flyers of its own--advising the French not to fraternize with blacks in the military. The sheet was ineffective.

Garret A. Morgan, a black scientist from Cleveland, Ohio, invented the smoke inhaler, better known as the "gas mask." It proved to be indispensable to the Allied Troops in WWI-- saving them from deadly German gas.

BACK ON THE HOME FRONT...

ANTI-NEGRO RIOTERS AGAIN PLY THE TORCH

Three More Bodies Found To-Day at East St. Louis, Making Total 27—Additional Troops May Be Sent There

Prisoners Given to Bloodthirsty Whites by Sheriff, Who Sees Them Lynched

TORCH LAW SANCTION

The Chicago Defender

SATURDAY, MAY 24, 1919

WANTED TO LEAVE FARM; IS LYNCHED

Dublin, Ga., May 23.—

who was sen

Thousands Are Driven From South at Point of Gun; Troops Aid Possemen

(By Century News Service)

Elaine, Ark., Oct. 10.—It was

essary to call

Negroes in the States moved North to work in the factories producing war supplies. Wherever they moved, racial violence followed.

In Europe, the Germans continued to throw atrocities in the faces of black soldiers in an effort to make them desert. The German campaign compelled President Wilson to officially denounce lynching (although no anti-lynching law was forthcoming).

In July 1917 a riot in East St. Louis, Illinois, ended with Negro homes burned and vandalized. 40 blacks and 8 whites were killed. The NAACP protested with a **Silent March** on New York's Fifth Avenue, on July 28, 1917. Black men in dark suits and women and children in white marched carrying banners, "Mr. President, why not make America safe for Democracy." The only sound was muffled drums.

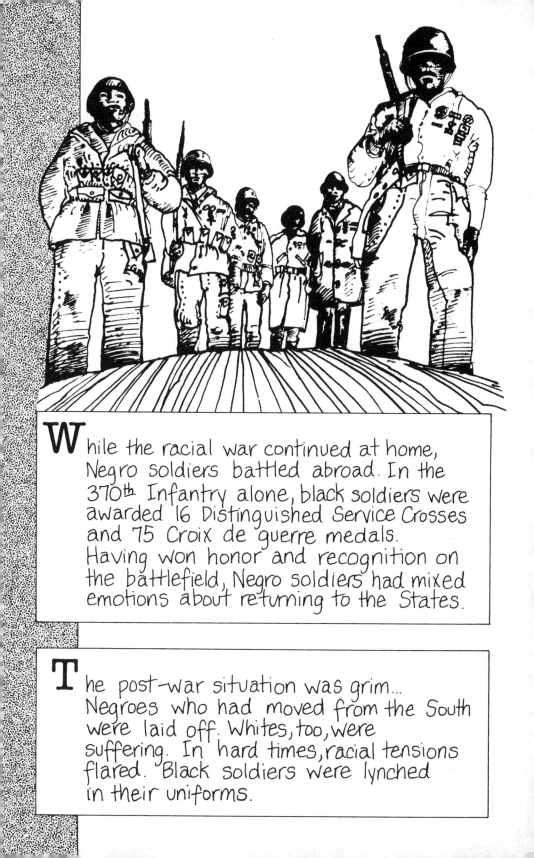

While the racial war continued at home, Negro soldiers battled abroad. In the 370th Infantry alone, black soldiers were awarded 16 Distinguished Service Crosses and 75 Croix de guerre medals. Having won honor and recognition on the battlefield, Negro soldiers had mixed emotions about returning to the States.

The post-war situation was grim... Negroes who had moved from the South were laid off. Whites, too, were suffering. In hard times, racial tensions flared. Black soldiers were lynched in their uniforms.

In 1919 there were more than 25 race riots in Longview, Texas; Knoxville, Tennessee; Omaha, Nebraska; Washington, D.C., and Chicago, Illinois.

The last two incidents moved President Wilson to remark that "the white race was the aggressor" and it "was more censurable because our Negro troops are but back from no little share in carrying our cause and our flag to victory "

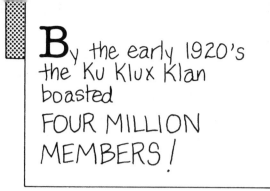

By the early 1920's the Ku Klux Klan boasted FOUR MILLION MEMBERS!

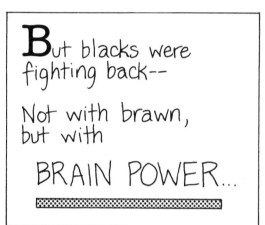

But blacks were fighting back--

Not with brawn, but with

BRAIN POWER...

Lenox Avenue: Midnight

The rhythm of life
Is a jazz rhythm,
Honey
The gods are laughing at us.

The broken heart of love,
The weary, weary heat of pain—
      Overtones,
      Undertones,
To the rumble of street cars,
To the swish of rain.

Lenox Avenue,
Honey
Midnight
And the gods are laughing at us.

                    —Langston Hughes

In the 1920's Negroes expressed themselves and their American experience through the arts --literature, music and studio arts. The movement, named for the Negro section of New York City, was known as The Harlem Renaissance.

These bold new artists dazzled the world...

EUBIE BLAKE & NOBLE SISSLE

DUKE ELLINGTON

Their names have become legend...

Deep feelings and keen perceptions emerged through the work of a new wave of poets and writers--Langston Hughes, Claude McKay, Countee Cullen, James Weldon Johnson, Jean Toomer, Jessie Faucet, and Rudolph Fisher.

More books were published by Negro authors during the 20's than in any other decade of American history.

Langston Hughes

Claude McKay

The writers of the Harlem Renaissance understood their history as blacks in America and the way it was woven into the social tapestry of the nation.

They took artistic action.

Not everyone wrote about "being black," but they were black and they were artists; that was—and is— a statement in itself.

Paul Robeson (left) and Charles Gilpin appeared in theatrical productions-- both in Eugene O'Neill's The Emperor Jones.

Eubie Blake, Noble Sissle, F.E. Miller and Aubrey Lyle wrote and produced the musical Shuffle Along in 1921—a huge New York success.

In 1923 Josephine Baker made her New York debut in Blake and Sissle's Chocolate Dandies.

Florence Mills (right) starred and dazzled audiences in Dixie to Broadway and Blackbirds (1924, 1926).

Composers W.C. Handy, J. Rosamond Johnson, and Harry J. Burleigh were writing and arranging Negro spirituals; Roland Hayes and the duet of Paul Robeson and Lawrence Brown were performing them.

Carter Woodson, the "Father of Black History," was the editor and leading force behind the <u>Journal of Negro History</u> for 35 years. The <u>Journal</u> was one of the earliest and most influential publications to dispel misconceptions and to chronicle the heritage of black people.

Born in 1875, Woodson was the son of uneducated former slaves. Through his own determination, Woodson became a teacher, administrator, and finally a leading historian.

James Weldon Johnson was born in Florida during Reconstruction. Educated in public schools, he later graduated from Atlanta University and returned to Jacksonville, Fla., to teach. He became Florida's first black attorney.

Fluent in Spanish, Johnson served as U.S. Counsel to Venezuela and Nicaragua by appointment of Theodore Roosevelt. He also served as first field secretary of the NAACP. His talents were not limited to the political arena. With his brother Rosamond and friend Bill Coles, he composed several Broadway musicals. His literary achievements include novels and poetry. Johnson and his brother are best remembered for "Lift Ev'ry Voice and Sing," the Negro National Anthem.

Langston Hughes was a writer who chose life experience over an academic education. After studying briefly at Columbia University, he worked on a series of ships, seeing Africa, Europe and the Canary Islands. Returning to New York in 1924, Hughes wrote prose and poetry combining images from his trips with the jazz rhythms of Harlem.

Katharine Dunham brought the dynamic grace of African ritual to modern dance. A dancer, anthropologist, ethnologist & choreographer, she revolutionized dance in the West. By studying the movement and symbolism of African ritual, she created dances that combine ballet, modern, and Afro-Cuban styles, known as "The Dunham Technique."

"Epilogue" by Langston Hughes

I, too, sing America

I am the darker brother
They send me to eat in the kitchen
When company comes,
But I laugh
and eat well
And grow strong

Tomorrow,
I'll sit at the table
When company comes.
Nobody'll dare
Say to me
"Eat in the kitchen"
Then.

Besides,
They'll see how beautiful I am
And be ashamed

I, too, am America

Charles Gilpin

"Jelly Roll" Morton

Billie Holliday

Harlem was chic, the place to be. The real significance of the Renaissance was that Negro artists were producing it, and, in doing so, educating the public.

Marcus Garvey believed that dark-skinned people belonged in their ancestral home —Africa. He envisioned a black empire and promoted black economic independence.

He organized the Universal Negro Improvement Association, organized a "Back-to-Africa" movement and gained a large following.

Garvey was the first to say "black is beautiful."

During the Depression, employment grew so scarce that whites began to take unskilled jobs traditionally held by blacks.

During these hard times a new organizational tool was born:
THE BOYCOTT.

Grocery stores and small businesses in black neighborhoods used white employees—in spite of black clientele. In 1933 the Citizen's League for Fair Play was organized and Rev. John H. Johnson of New York City persuaded white merchants to use black clerks.
The tactic was: "Don't Buy Where You Can't Work." The result was that hundreds of blacks got jobs in Harlem and with the public utilities.

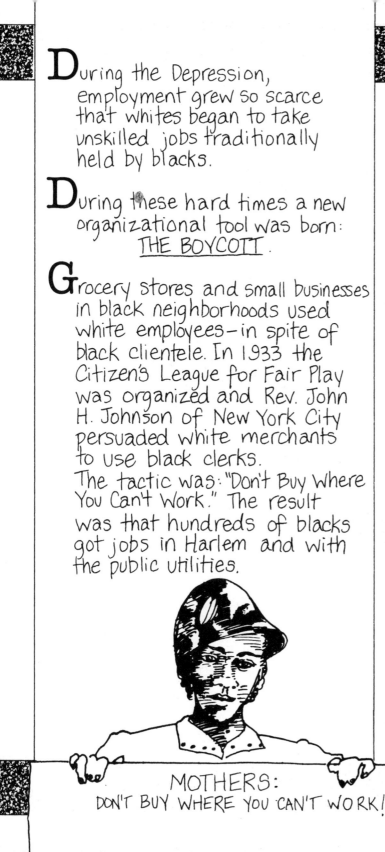

MOTHERS:
DON'T BUY WHERE YOU CAN'T WORK!

Around 1924, black people began to shift their allegiance from the Republican party to the Democratic.

During the 1928 presidential campaign, black newspapers supported Democrat Al Smith rather than Herbert Hoover.

A major victory came to pass in 1930 when blacks opposed J.J. Parker's confirmation to the U.S. Supreme Court.
The Senate appropriately rejected Parker.

The presidency of Franklin Delano Roosevelt clinched the black migration to the Democratic Party.

New Deal policies were designed for the unemployed common man and woman.

Each New Deal program and agency had a different effect on blacks. Some were more beneficial than others.

 = National Youth Administration

Mary McLeod Bethune was appointed to head the N.Y.A. division of Negro affairs. In the student work program alone there were 64,000 young black people.

 = Civilian Conservation Corps

The C.C.C. employed 200,000 young blacks.

 = Work Projects Administration

The W.P.A. employed approximately a million black people in jobs ranging from secretaries to artists. It fostered the Chicago Renaissance, providing opportunities for artists like painter Charles White.

 = Federal Writers' Project

The F.W.P. saw the emergence of novelist, folklorist, and story writer Zora Neal Hurston, and of novelist Richard Wriston.

It was Eleanor Roosevelt, more than FDR, who won the confidence of blacks. A friend of Mary McLeod Bethune, educator and founder of Bethune-Cookman College, Mrs. Roosevelt kept the President in touch with black issues.

She raised eyebrows when she invited the Council of Negro Women to the White House.

Mrs. Roosevelt's most dramatic stroke came in 1939, when the Daughters of the American Revolution blocked

acclaimed soprano Marian Anderson from singing in Constitution Hall. Mrs. Roosevelt withdrew her membership from the club. The concert took place outside the Lincoln Memorial.

FDR consulted experts in a number of fields and added black advisors to his prestigious ranks. This "black brain trust" worked to see that economic strength through employment—specifically in government—was made available to blacks.

FDR's Black Cabinet: Mary McLeod Bethune is standing in the center of the front row.

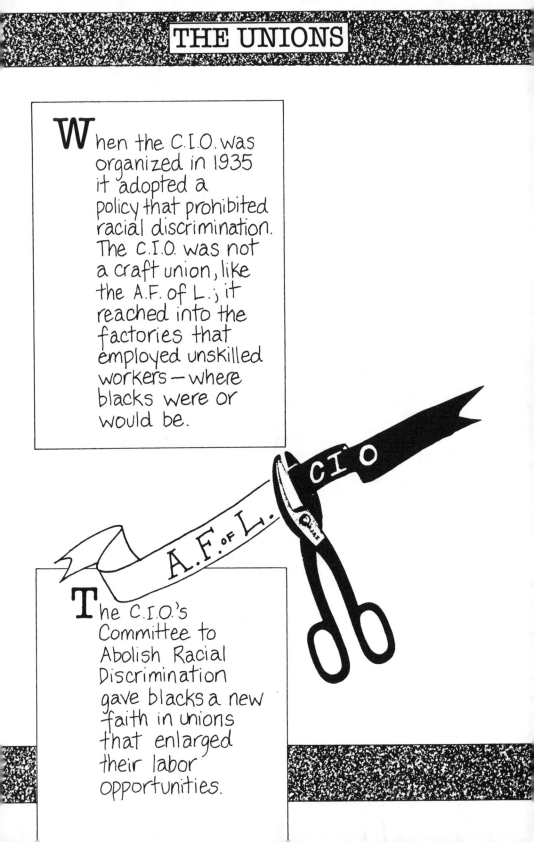

When the C.I.O. was organized in 1935 it adopted a policy that prohibited racial discrimination. The C.I.O. was not a craft union, like the A.F. of L.; it reached into the factories that employed unskilled workers — where blacks were or would be.

The C.I.O.'s Committee to Abolish Racial Discrimination gave blacks a new faith in unions that enlarged their labor opportunities.

A. Philip Randolph fought the Pullman Company for 12 years. He organized the Brotherhood of Sleeping Car Porters and saw that they were recognized as a union.

In 1941 Randolph planned a march on Washington of 100,000 blacks unless FDR did something to end discrimination in the war industries. In order to avoid the demonstration, Roosevelt issued Executive Order 8802, which snuffed out discrimination in Randolph's targeted industries. FDR later appointed a Fair Employment Practices Committee to see that the Executive Order was properly enforced.

When Japan attacked Pearl Harbor on December 7, 1941, a black sailor named **Dorie Miller** was on the tragic Arizona. Like all blacks in Uncle Sam's Navy, Miller was limited to the messman detail. When Japan struck, though, Miller turned the Arizona's guns skyward and fired endlessly. His heroic action precipitated the charge in navy policy that cleared the way for black naval officers.

The U. S. Army and Navy remained **segregated** during World War II. 1,154,720 blacks were drafted. This time, however, black enlisted men, women and officers had no illusions about their war effort changing race prejudices at home. In fact, a few riots, similar to those during W W I period, broke out in Detroit, Michigan; Beaumont, Texas; and New York.

"The nation cannot expect colored people to feel that the United States is worth defending if the Negro continues to be treated as he (and she) is."

MRS. ROOSEVELT

One major change happened after World War II. Black leaders like A.P. Randolph, William Hastie, and Thurgood Marshall pressed to have the armed forces de-segregated. President Harry Truman issued an Executive Order demanding "equal treatment" and equal opportunity in the armed forces.

Black Americans distinguished themselves on the battlefields. As civilians, they were on draft boards, in factories, and in numerous volunteer organizations.

President Truman wanted to prevent the kind of post-war backlash that contaminated the U.S. after the First World War. In 1946 he appointed an interracial civil rights committee, including the distinguished black woman attorney Sadie T.M. Alexander. The committee's report, To Secure These Rights, proposed that the abolishment of segregation was essential in ensuring equal and just civil rights.

The post-World War II atmosphere was more hopeful for blacks than had been anticipated.

The 1950's and 1960's were kaleidoscopic with changing images of the black experience...

Lieutenant L. Martin
Army Nurse Corps, Tokyo.

William Hastie:
First black judge—
U.S. Circuit Court
of Appeals.

Gwendolyn Brooks,
a poet and
novelist, receives
the Pulitzer
Prize.

Ralph Bunche
receives Nobel
Peace Prize.

Jackie Robinson & Roy Campanella play on mixed baseball teams in the south.

"Concerning our children's minds there is no place for local option"
— Thurgood Marshall

Through the painstaking and nonstop efforts of the NAACP, segregation in schools was attacked—resulting in the Brown vs. Board of Education Decision in 1954. At last, with this decision, "separate but equal" public schools were declared unconstitutional.

President Eisenhower, in spite of his personal opinions, upheld the highest U.S. Court's ruling. He was aware that, as leader of the "free world," the United States could not renege.

 **MAY 17, 1954 :** Racial segregation is outlawed in public schools (Brown vs. Board of Education).

 **MAY 31, 1955 :** Educational integration to be achieved with "all deliberate speed" (2nd Brown vs Board of Education Decision).

 **MARCH 5, 1956 :** Ban on segregation applied also to tax-supported colleges and universities.

In 1957 the Supreme Court ruling was challenged in Little Rock, Arkansas.

When nine black teen-agers tried to register at Little Rock's Central High, Governor Faubus barred their admittance.

He posted State National Guards in front of the school.

It took a Supreme Court edict, a presidential proclamation, the 101st Army Airborne Division AND a special Federalized state militia to escort the students to school.

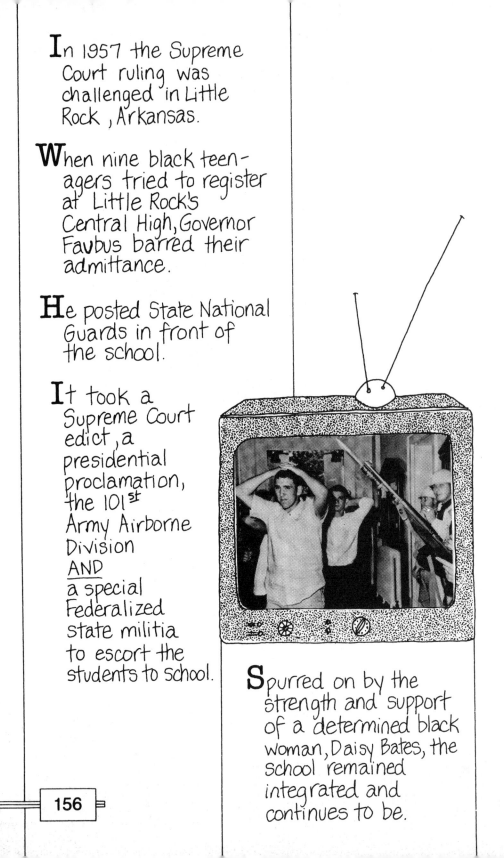

Spurred on by the strength and support of a determined black woman, Daisy Bates, the school remained integrated and continues to be.

Television entered the average American home during the '50's—and the "race question" in images.

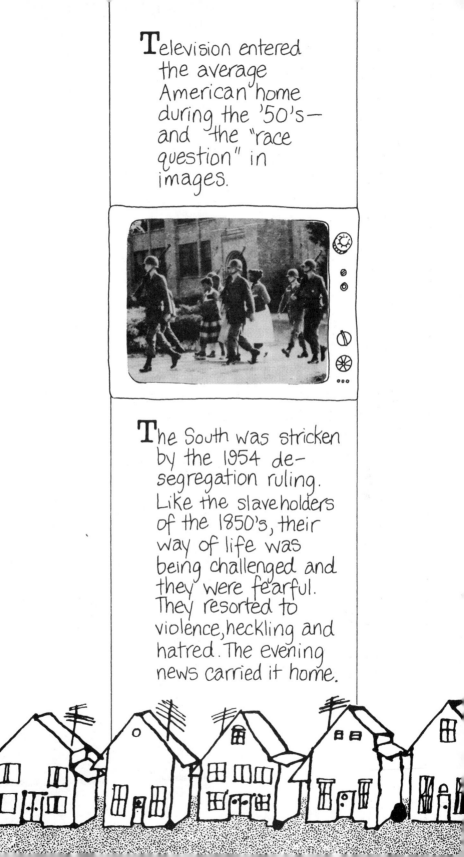

The South was stricken by the 1954 de-segregation ruling. Like the slaveholders of the 1850's, their way of life was being challenged and they were fearful. They resorted to violence, heckling and hatred. The evening news carried it home.

Spurred on by the strength of many determined souls, the struggle had its victories.

James Meredith enters U. of Mississippi, 1962

Y G. McMAHON
DEAN.
E LAW SCHOOL

Roy Wilson: 1ST black to enter U. of Louisiana, 1950

George McLaurin and wife attend Oklahoma U.

It was
a time
of
consciousness-
raising
in
America...

Black leaders like Dr. Martin
Luther King emerged with a
new tactic-influenced by Gandhi-
of nonviolent civil disobedience.
King believed in the power of
people gathered together.

Just as true believers in
American idealism advanced
the abolition movement
a century before, black and
white Americans in the '60's
expressed their fervor and
belief in equality and
freedom in the Civil
Rights Movement.

ithin the next decade, four major tactics distinguished the movement for Civil Rights:

1. BOYCOTTS

2. SIT-INS

3. FREEDOM RIDES

4. MASS MARCHES

One month before the Brown Decision, a young, Atlanta-born D.D. candidate from Boston University — Dr. Martin Luther King — accepted the pastorship of Montgomery, Alabama's Dexter Avenue Baptist Church.

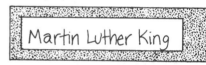

Martin Luther King

In 1955, the first year of Dr. King's return south, a 14-year-old black youth from Chicago, Illinois, made another journey south to Greenwood, Mississippi. His name was Emmet Till. Because Till allegedly whistled at a white woman, he was murdered and tossed into the Tallahatchie River, weighed down by a 75-lb. cotton gin fan tied to his neck with barbed wire.

Emmet Till

Senseless murders of Negroes weren't unusual in Jim Crow land, but Till's death came at a pivotal moment in history, and both black and white Americans denouced the crime. **The church**—heart, vein and artery of the black community—and church leaders **aroused their congregations**. Dr. King's articulate baritone was among the booming voices. His social awareness and powerful preaching caught the attention of **E. D. Nixon**, who lead Alabama's NAACP.

Nixon believed that Montgomery's bus ordinances could be challenged in court and was on the alert for a case to take to the Supreme Court, as Marshall had done. **70% of Montgomery's bus passengers were black,** but **none** of the drivers were. **Blacks had to pay their fare at the front door but enter and sit in the back** and give their seats to white passengers when buses were full. Busdrivers harassed black riders and often pulled away while blacks walked from the coin box to the back door.

On December 2, 1955, Rosa Parks, a former secretary of the local NAACP, quietly but firmly refused to relinquish her seat on the bus to a white passenger.

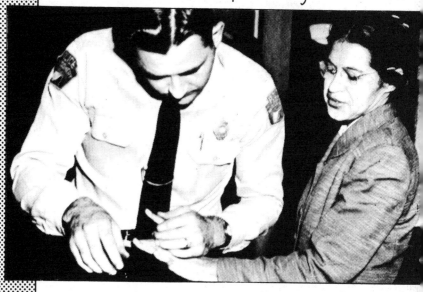

When she was arrested and charged with violating the city ordinance, she wisely called E.D. Nixon. He met with King and other church leaders. Three days later, the Montgomery Bus Boycott had begun, directed by the newly-formed Montgomery Improvement Association, with Dr. King as its president.

To city officials, compliance with the Association's demands would threaten to destroy the social fabric of the segregated South and was therefore unthinkable.

The boycott would persist until:

1. Bus drivers were courteous.

2. Passengers were seated on a first-come, first served basis.

3. Black drivers were employed for predominantly black routes.

As one elderly woman put it, "I'm not walkin' for myself, I'm walkin' for my children and grandchildren."

By March 1956, the boycott was still in effect and King was placed on trial. In June, Alabama's law was declared unconstitutional by a federal court. The final triumph came on November 13th, 1956, when the U.S. Supreme Court upheld the decision of the lower court and outlawed Alabama's bus segregation laws, effective December 20, 1956. Other bus boycotts followed the victory.

From Boycott to Ballot:

The Southern Christian Leadership Conference was formed after the success of the Montgomery boycott. While the NAACP fought legal battles in the courts, SCLC involved masses of grass-roots people in peaceful confrontation. King, a disciple of Gandhi, believed that non-violent civil disobedience was the most powerful weapon for confronting discrimination.

"The objective was not to coerce but to correct, not to break bodies or wills but to move hearts."
—M.L.King

I n 1958, Negro leaders met with President Eisenhower requesting that he submit new Civil Rights legislation to Congress and openly pledge to support the Brown decision.

E isenhower did not respond. Like most Americans he hadn't given much thought to the "Negro Question" and did not regard it as a pressing issue. He accepted the status quo.

As the 1960 Presidential Election approached, Civil Rights emerged as a major issue. King wisely noted that "...the most decisive steps the Negro can take... is that short walk to the voting booth." In October,

one month before the election, King was arrested during a sit-in in Atlanta. He was sentenced to 4 months' hard labor at the Reidsville Penitentiary, 300 miles from Atlanta, deep in Klan country.

Senator John F. Kennedy made his first overt move on Civil Rights by calling King's wife with a promise to help. Robert Kennedy followed with a call to the officiating judge, who reversed his decision and released King on a $2,000 bond.

W

ithout making an official endorsement, King publicly acknowledged Kennedy's "courage" and "principles" as a "great force" behind his release. With 75% of the Negro vote, Kennedy won the election by a slim margin.

← Vote

President John F. Kennedy was an idealist who educated himself about blacks in America. His "New Frontier" expressed optimism, and young white students were inspired by it.

Boycotts spread through the South. By the early '60's, college students began to sit in segregated stores and public places. "Sit-ins" were another form of non-violent protest and they too spread through the south.

On February 2, 1960, 4 students from North Carolina's 'A&T College in Greensboro sat at Woolworth's lunch counter. In spite of insults and threats, they resolved not to leave until they were served. The following week, having made return visits daily, they were still waiting. They were joined by students—black and white—from nearby colleges.

In less than two weeks sit-ins had spread across the South. More than 500 people gathered at a Nashville lunch counter. Soon department stores, libraries and public facilities were scenes for sit-ins challenging Jim Crow laws once again. Television made the protests visible to an international audience. The student Non-Violent Coordinating Committee (SNCC) was the organization behind the sit-ins.

Segregated buses had been declared unconstitutional, but Jim Crow persisted. In May 1961, the Congress of Racial Equality (CORE), led by James Farmer, launched "Freedom Rides." Two buses with integrated passengers embarked from Washington, D.C., headed for New Orleans.

The first bus was set on fire, the second was attacked by the Klan. Attorney General **Robert Kennedy** replaced the buses with a third one. When the riders reached Montgomery, Alabama, bedlam broke loose and RFK sent federal marshalls. (The governor of Alabama refused to send the National Guard.) During the summer, more than **400 Freedom riders were arrested and three freedom riders were murdered.**

When RFK suggested a cooling-off period, Farmer replied, "We have been cooling off for 100 years..."

James Farmer

By the fall, the attorney general advised the ICC to issue regulations desegregating interstate busing facilities —effective November 1, 1961.

5 Freedom Riders jailed in Montgomery, Alabama May 1961.

James Zeig was beaten and left bleeding while white ambulance drivers refused to help.

The next wave in the move for Civil Rights was voter registration. The drive was met with violence and resistance in the South, but black and white college students persisted in registering blacks. With SNCC and CORE at the helm, Bobby Kennedy established the Voter Education Project.

In February 1963 JFK presented a new Civil Rights bill to Congress. Lacking a public mandate, it failed. One year later, the bill was passed. In the wake of President Kennedy's death, it was a tribute to him.

On August 28, 1963, the Civil Rights Bill received a stirring mandate. 250,000 people marched to the Lincoln Memorial—black and white, rich and poor, educated and non-educated, movie stars and garbage collectors. The throng swayed to the anthem of the movement, "We Shall Overcome."

King gave his "I have a dream" speech. That dream, of a nation where people are judged by "the content of their character, rather than by the color of their skin," has yet to be realized.

In JFK's words, "Now the time has come for this nation to fulfill its promise... Those who do nothing are inviting shame as well as violence."

The violence came in the form of urban riots cries of "burn, baby, burn," born out of frustration in black ghettos.

As blacks sought solutions, different movements evolved offering various tactics & beliefs.

Malcolm X, the proud and eloquent Black Muslim spokesman, formed the Organization of Afro-American Unity.

The Black Muslims are a religious group which began in 1929 when Elijah Muhammed (then Elijah Poole) saw Allah in the street.

Muslims believe in Allah and a "build black, buy black" kind of self-sufficiency. In 1968 Muslims put a million dollars into Chicago's South side ghetto. There they have created their own community with Muslim stores, restaurants, farms and temples.

Constantly faced with the business end of a gun or billy club forced some to advocate armed revolution.

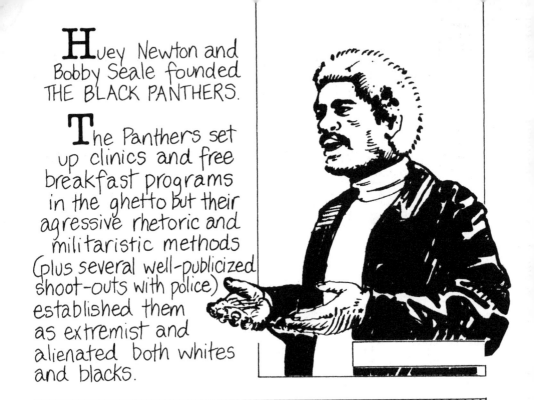

Huey Newton and Bobby Seale founded THE BLACK PANTHERS.

The Panthers set up clinics and free breakfast programs in the ghetto but their agressive rhetoric and militaristic methods (plus several well-publicized shoot-outs with police) established them as extremist and alienated both whites and blacks.

REMEMBER the POPULISTS

POOR M_

In 1968 King began to organize a "Poor People's Campaign," and planned a march on Washington, D.C.

The disadvantaged of all races would ask with one voice why their rights had been ignored.

President Lyndon Johnson proved to be a friend of Civil Rights, championing a new Civil Rights Bill and Voting Rights Act.

Senator Robert Kennedy had grown in his understanding of problems facing black Americans and earned their confidence and support.

King was murdered in 1968.
In his last speech, he said:
"I have been to the mountain top and I have seen the promised land...

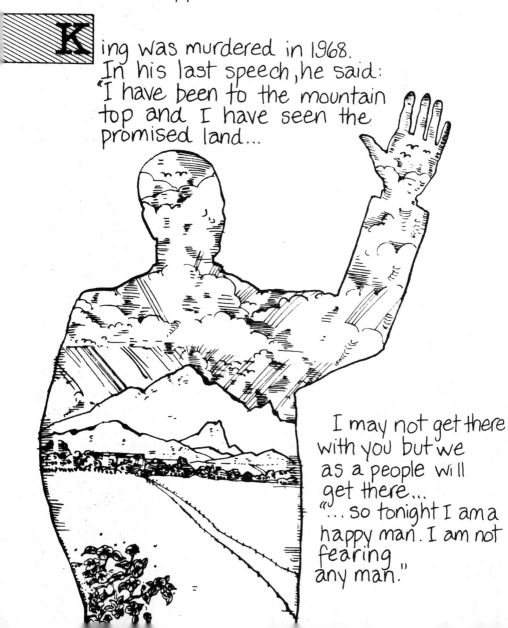

I may not get there with you but we as a people will get there...
"... so tonight I am a happy man. I am not fearing any man."

1970's

Gains of the preceding decades were set in motion. Through the Affirmative Action and Equal Opportunity programs, qualified blacks were recruited by colleges and the job market.

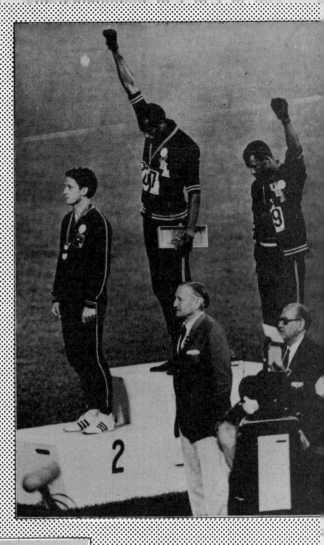

Black legislators organized the Congressional Black Caucus, which was designed to address the needs of all minorities.

Carl Stokes, the first black mayor of a major U.S. city—Cleveland—was joined by Richard Hatcher (Gary, Indiana), Thomas Bradley (Los Angeles, California) and Maynard Jackson (Atlanta, Georgia).

The number of black
mayors increased
throughout the decade:

- Walter Washington
- Richard Hatcher
- Maynard Jackson

The Reverend
Jesse Jackson, a
protégé of Martin
Luther King, founded
P.U.S.H. —
People United to
Save Humanity —
a black self-help
group.

The end of the 1970's, like that of the 1870's, marked the beginning of a backlash curtailing black achievements.

The election of Ronald Reagan can be compared with that of Rutherford B. Hayes. Both administrations withdrew moral and legislative support from programs that ensured social and economic justice for blacks; both men wooed voters who believed that their success depended on the failure of blacks.

The
1980's
pose a
challenge...

"I refuse to accept the cynical notion that nation after nation must spiral down...into the hell of nuclear destruction. I believe that unarmed truth and unconditional love will have the final word in reality."

—Martin Luther King, 1964
Nobel Prize Acceptance

Black Americans are proof that people can change even the most horrendous circumstances. Black history is a lesson and an inspiration.

BIBLIOGRAPHY

This book serves as an accessible, open door for those who seek a foundation of knowledge and understanding about this provocative and powerful branch of human history. The bibliography is designed to assist those who want to build on the foundation that has been set by Black History for Beginners

Allen, James S. Reconstruction—The Battle for Democracy.
    New York: International Publishers, 1937

Aptheker, Herbert. Essays in the History of the American Negro.
    New York: International Publishers, 1964.

Bennett, Lerone. Before the Mayflower.
    Chicago: Johnson Publications, Inc., 1964.

Bennett, Lerone. The Shaping of Black America.
    Chicago: Johnson Publications, Inc., 1975.

Carmichael, Stockley, and Charles V. Hamilton. Black Power.
    New York: Knopf, Inc., 1967.

Cleaver, Eldridge. Soul On Ice.
    New York: McGraw-Hill, 1968.

Daniel, Peter. Shadow of Slavery: Peonage in the South.
    New York: Oxford University Press, 1972.

Davidson, Basil. The African Slave Trade.
    Boston-Toronto: Little, Brown and Co., 1961.

Douglass, Frederick. My Bondage and My Freedom.
    New York: Dover Publications, 1969.

DuBois, W.E.B. The Souls of Black Folk.
    Scarborough, Ontario: New American Library of
    Canada, Ltd., 1969.

Franklin, John Hope. From Slavery to Freedom: A History of
    Negro America.
    New York: Knopf, 1974.

Gutman, Herbert G. The Black Family in Slavery and
    Freedom.
    New York: Random House, 1976.

Gwaltney, John Langston. Drylongso.
    New York: Vintage Books, 1981.

Haley, Alex and Malcolm X. The Autobiography of
    Malcolm X.
    New York: Grove Press, 1965.

Harris, Levitt, Furman, Smith, eds. The Black Book.
    New York: Random House, 1974.

Higginbotham. A. Leon. The Matter of Color.
    New York: Oxford University Press, 1978.

Huggins, Nathan Irvin. Voices from the Harlem Renaissance.
    New York: Oxford University Press, 1976.

James, Lowenberg and Bogin. Black Women in 19th Century
    American Life.
    University Park and London: Pennsylvania State
    University Press, 1976.

Morrison-Reed, Mark D. Black Pioneers.
    Boston: Beacon Press, 1980.

Mullen, Robert W. Blacks in American Wars.
New York: Pathfinder Press, 1973.

Oates, Stephen B. Let the Trumpet Sound.
New York: Harper & Row, 1982.

Still, William. The Underground Railroad.
Chicago: Johnson Publications, Inc., 1970.

Williams, Eric. Capitalism and Slavery.
North Carolina: University of North Carolina Press, 1944.

Williams, Larraine A. Africa and the Afro-American
Experience.
Washington, D.C.: Howard University Press, 1977.

ACKNOWLEDGEMENTS

J. Bowen, D. Cattell, Q. Cattell, R. Elmore, M. Horwitz,
V. Juhasz, R. Kelso, S. Willmarth; my agent,
Marian Young Straus and publisher,
Glenn Thompson—Thanks.

The text of this book is dedicated in memory of:

My parents, Norman and Harriette Dennis, whose knowledge made history a natural part of our home life
and
My great-great-great grandfather, Printz Perkins who, in 1792, established a settlement of free blacks like himself, on his property in Susquehanna County, northeastern Pennsylvania.

To the living:

Edith Dennis Moore and Lon for their love and support

—Denise Dennis